EXTREME SCIENCE

SPECTACULAR LIGHT AND SOUND

WAYLAND
www.waylandbooks.co.uk

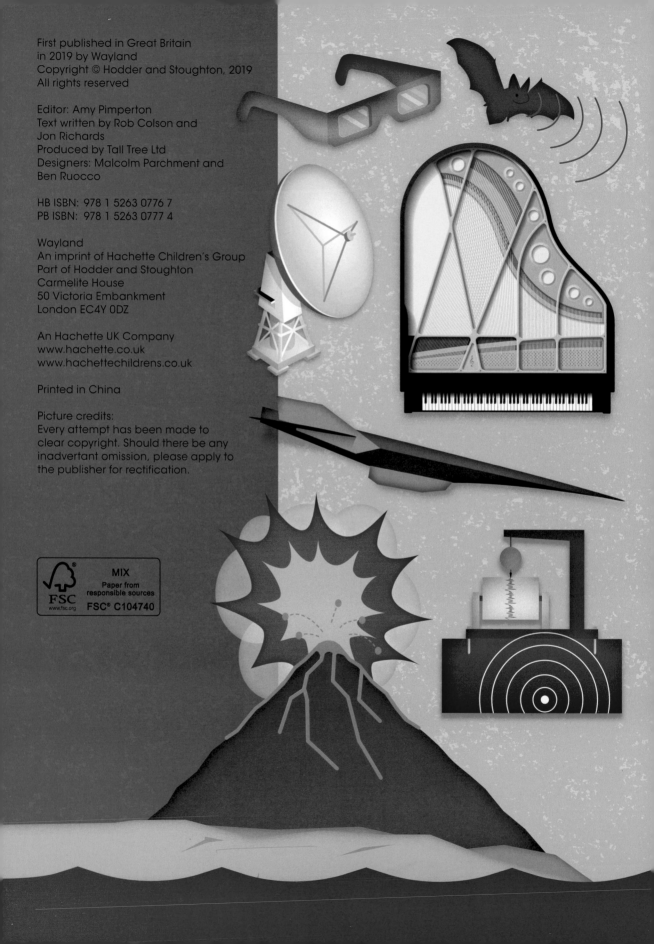

First published in Great Britain
in 2019 by Wayland

Editor: Amy Pimperton
Text written by Rob Colson and
Jon Richards
Produced by Tall Tree Ltd
Designers: Malcolm Parchment and
Ben Ruocco

HB ISBN: 978 1 5263 0776 7
PB ISBN: 978 1 5263 0777 4

Wayland
An imprint of Hachette Children's Group
Part of Hodder and Stoughton
Carmelite House
50 Victoria Embankment
London EC4Y 0DZ

An Hachette UK Company
www.hachette.co.uk
www.hachettechildrens.co.uk

Printed in China

Picture credits:
Every attempt has been made to
clear copyright. Should there be any
inadvertant omission, please apply to
the publisher for rectification.

CONTENTS

WHAT IS LIGHT?

Light is a form of energy that travels in waves. The Sun is the main source of the light that we can see, but there are lots of other light sources, including electric lights and even animals.

VISIBLE LIGHT

The light that we can see and all its colours is known as the visible spectrum. It forms a small part of the electromagnetic spectrum, which also contains invisible forms of energy, such as infrared and X-rays. Light rays travel in straight lines, but they can be bent when they pass from one material to another.

Angle of refraction

White light

Red
Orange
Yellow
Green
Blue
Indigo
Violet

BENDING LIGHT

The white light that we see from the Sun is made up of all the colours of the rainbow! If light passes through a prism, it is separated out into its different colours.

When light passes through a prism, it is refracted (bent). Each colour bends at a slightly different angle.

REFLECTING LIGHT

Objects have a colour because they absorb all the other colours, and reflect only that particular colour. A red ball will reflect red light, but absorb all the other colours of light.

Colour spectrum

This ball reflects red light and absorbs all other colours.

ELECTRIC AND MAGNETIC

Light travels through space as a wave of energy. There are two parts to the wave: an electric field and a magnetic field at right angles to the electric field. The distance between each peak of a wave is called the **wavelength**. The wavelength of visible light ranges from violet at **380 billionths** of a metre to red at **750 billionths** of a metre.

Electric field

Wavelength

Peak

Magnetic field

Direction of wave travel

The number of complete cycles of light that pass through one point in a second is called the

FREQUENCY.

Visible light has a frequency of more than 400 trillion cycles per second!

5

Light takes 8 minutes to reach us from the Sun.

SPEED OF LIGHT

Light is the fastest thing in the Universe, and travels at a speed of just under **300,000 km** a second. In one year, light travels **9.5 trillion km**. This distance is called a light year, and astronomers use it as a unit to measure the extreme distances across space. The closest star to our Sun is **Proxima Centauri**, which is **4.22 light years** from Earth.

Sun

BRIGHTEST

While your bedroom lights might seem bright when they're turned on first thing in the morning, there are plenty of even brighter objects that are really out of this world.

MEASURING BRIGHTNESS

Astronomers measure the brightness of objects in space using magnitude. An object's actual brightness is called its absolute magnitude.

However, an object's brightness will get dimmer the further away it is. A super-bright object that is millions of light years away may appear as a dim smudge in the night sky. How bright an object appears to someone standing on Earth is called its apparent magnitude.

MAGNITUDE SCALE

Apparent magnitude is measured in a scale. The brighter an object, the lower its value of apparent magnitude. These are the nine brightest objects in the sky, with their values of apparent magnitude.

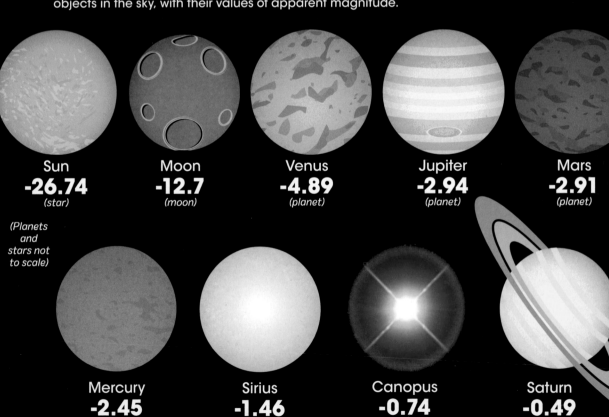

Sun
-26.74
(star)

Moon
-12.7
(moon)

Venus
-4.89
(planet)

Jupiter
-2.94
(planet)

Mars
-2.91
(planet)

(Planets and stars not to scale)

Mercury
-2.45
(planet)

Sirius
-1.46
(star)

Canopus
-0.74
(star)

Saturn
-0.49
(planet)

LASER LIGHT

Scientists have created a laser with a light that's about one billion times brighter than the Sun.

It could be used in medical equipment or to create powerful computer chips.

The Sun appears 13 billion times brighter in the sky than Sirius, which is the next-brightest star. Sirius has an absolute magnitude 25 times greater than that of the Sun.

WARNING: Never look directly at the Sun! It can permanently damage your eyesight.

The only safe way to look at the Sun is when wearing special solar eclipse glasses.

MAKING OR REFLECTING

Stars shine because they produce their own light. Planets and moons shine with light that is reflected from a light source, such as a nearby star.

Moon

Reflected light

Light made by the Sun

Sun

Earth

BRIGHTEST LIGHT

In 2016, astronomers detected a supernova (a massive star exploding at the end of its life) producing light that is about **570 billion** times brighter than the Sun, or 20 times brighter than all the stars in our galaxy, the Milky Way. This is the brightest light ever discovered.

DARKEST

Darkness is an absence of light. Some objects create darkness by blocking rays of light, while others are able to absorb light completely, creating mysterious black regions in space.

CASTING SHADOWS

Objects that are opaque don't let light pass through them. Because light travels in straight lines, a dark region called a shadow, or umbra, is created behind the object. Around this area of total shadow, there may be a fuzzy region of half-shadow, known as the penumbra.

8

Penumbra: the area of half-shade around the edges of a shadow, where a few light rays reach

Umbra: the area of total shade at the middle of a shadow, where no light rays reach

Object blocking light rays

Rays of light from light source

Light source

Normal black paint looks dark because it absorbs between **95-98 per cent** of the light that hits it. However, scientists have made a super-dark material called **Vantablack** that's made from carbon nanotubes. This amazing stuff can absorb **99.96 per cent** of the light that hits it, making it the darkest material ever made.

ECLIPSES

Eclipses occur when one astronomical object passes in front of a star, blocking light from that star. Solar eclipses occur when the Moon passes between the Sun and Earth, throwing a shadow onto Earth's surface.

There are three types of solar eclipse: **total** eclipses, **partial** eclipses and **annular** eclipses.

The earliest total solar eclipse ever recorded took place in

1374 BCE

in ancient Mesopotamia (modern-day Kurdistan).

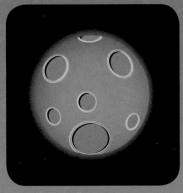

Total eclipse:
Moon totally hides the Sun

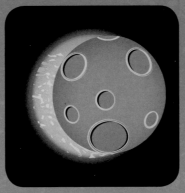

Partial eclipse:
Moon leaves a crescent
of Sun still showing

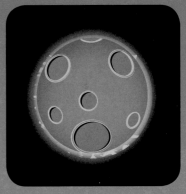

Annular eclipse:
Moon is further from Earth,
Sun forms a ring around Moon

A **sundial** tells the time by casting a shadow from a vertical gnomon. As the Sun moves across the sky, the shadow moves around the dial.

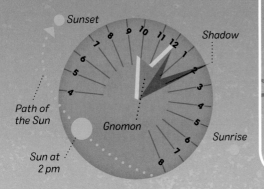

Sunset

Shadow

Path of
the Sun

Gnomon

Sunrise

Sun at
2 pm

During an eclipse, the shadow cast by the Moon onto Earth follows a belt-shaped path about **160 km** wide and **16,000 km** long.

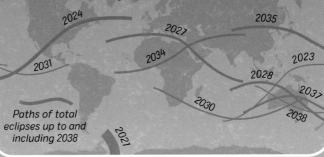

Paths of total
eclipses up to and
including 2038

Black hole

The darkest objects in the Universe are black holes, which are created when massive stars collapse in on themselves. These are regions of space that are so dense and have such strong gravity that nothing can escape them – not even light. Because of this, you cannot actually see a black hole, but you can detect one from its effects on objects around it.

VISION RANGES

The average human can detect about 1 million different colours that make up the visible spectrum. But there are animals out there with the power to see and detect forms of light that are invisible to us.

HUMAN VISION

Some people are **tetrachromats**, which means that they are able to detect **10 million colours** or more. People who are colour blind are called **dichromats** – they can only see about **10,000 colours**.

RODS AND CONES

Humans have two types of light-sensitive cells (**photoreceptors**) in their eyes. These are called **rods** and **cones**. Rods are sensitive to dim light and black and white shades, whereas cones detect colours.

There are three different types of cone photoreceptors, which detect different colours in the visible spectrum. People who are dichromats are missing one of the three kinds of cone.

A person who is red-green colour blind won't be able to see the number 12 here.

DISTANT LIGHT

On a dark night, your eyes could spot the light of a candle more than **45 km** away – if you could see round the curve of the Earth. Standing at sea level and looking across to the horizon, we can usually see about **5 km** away because Earth curves away from us. We can see the tops of tall ships from a greater distance.

The most distant object you can see without using a telescope is the Andromeda Galaxy, which is **2.6 million light years away.**

5 km

Person can only see the top of the ship.

20 km

Bluebottle butterfly

SUPER-VISION

Some animals have many more types of light-sensitive cones than humans, and can detect light that is invisible to us. Many reptiles and birds can see ultraviolet, while some snakes can sense infrared. Other animals, such as dogs, can only see a small range of colours.

Mantis shrimps have possibly the best eyesight of all. They have **12 types** of **photoreceptor**. It is thought that some colours are associated with detecting food.

Mantis shrimp eyes are very sensitive to ultraviolet.

Bumblebees are able to see **ultraviolet light**, which helps them locate nectar. However, they cannot see red!

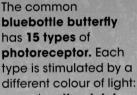

The common **bluebottle butterfly** has **15 types** of **photoreceptor.** Each type is stimulated by a different colour of light:

- **one** by **ultraviolet**
- **one** by violet
- **three** by shades of **blue**
- **one** by **blue-green**
- **four** by **green**
- **five** by **red** light.

Pit vipers can sense infrared using special pits in the sides of their heads. Infrared is given off by warm bodies, and the snakes can detect body heat from prey up to **one metre** away.

Sensory pit

INVISIBLE EXTREMES

Beyond the ranges of visible light are invisible forms of radiation that we can use to explore the edges of the Universe, see inside bodies ... and even cook food.

SHORT AND LONG

Gamma rays have the shortest wavelengths, which can be as small as **1 picometre** (one trillionth, or 1×10^{-12}, of a metre).

Radio waves have the longest wavelengths, which can measure more than **100 km** long.

FROM LOW TO HIGH

The wavelength of radiation can range from the width of a single atom to the length of an entire galaxy or longer. All light travels at the same speed, so the longer the wavelength, the lower the frequency.

LOWER

ENERGY LEVELS

RADIO WAVES
**Wavelength:
10 cm and longer**
Used to carry radio and TV signals, to communicate over long distances and to send GPS signals from satellites in orbit. Astronomers use large radio dishes to collect radio waves from objects far out in space.

MICROWAVES
Wavelength: 1 mm–10 cm
Used to carry mobile phone signals and to cook food.

1 nm (1 nanometre) equals one billionth of a metre.

INFRARED
**Wavelength
700 nm–1 mm**
Given off by warm objects, such as radiators.

PROTECTIVE SHIELD

Some parts of the electromagnetic spectrum are harmful to us. Fortunately, Earth's atmosphere blocks parts of this harmful radiation, including high-energy gamma rays that can damage living tissues. Some space telescopes are tuned to detect the radiation that does not reach the surface.

We are protected from the most harmful forms of ultraviolet light by a layer of the gas **OZONE** between 20 and 30 km above the surface of Earth.

VISIBLE LIGHT

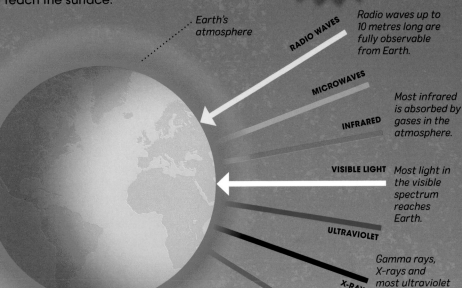

Earth's atmosphere

RADIO WAVES — Radio waves up to 10 metres long are fully observable from Earth.

MICROWAVES

INFRARED — Most infrared is absorbed by gases in the atmosphere.

VISIBLE LIGHT — Most light in the visible spectrum reaches Earth.

ULTRAVIOLET

X-RAY

GAMMA RADIATION — Gamma rays, X-rays and most ultraviolet rays are blocked by the upper atmosphere, and can only be observed from space.

HIGHER

ULTRAVIOLET
Wavelength: 10 nm–400 nm
Produced by the Sun, this radiation warms Earth and causes sunburn. It is used to spot forged bank notes.

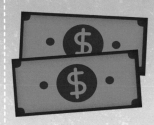

X-RAYS
Wavelength: 0.1 nm–10 nm
Energetic X-rays can pass through soft tissues in the body, and are used to produce 'pictures' of hard tissue, such as bones.

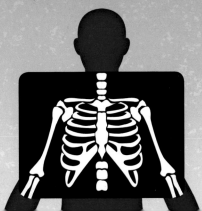

GAMMA RAYS
Wavelength: under 0.1 nm
A powerful and dangerous form of energy that is the most energetic type of electromagnetic radiation. It is used to irradiate food (killing bacteria) and in forms of radiation cancer treatment.

SEEING THE IMPOSSIBLE

To study objects that we can't see with the naked eye, we build microscopes that can view the minute world of individual atoms, or send telescopes out into space to study galaxies as they were when the Universe was born!

FOCUSING LIGHT

Telescopes and **microscopes** collect light from objects and bring it into focus to produce a sharp image.

Dutch scientist **Antonie Van Leeuwenhoek (1632–1723)** was the first person to see **bacteria** under a microscope.

A LIGHT MICROSCOPE

uses a lens or several lenses to collect light from an object and focus it.

Eyepiece lens

Magnifying lens

Magnified object

Object

REFLECTOR TELESCOPES

collect light using mirrors.

The largest ever reflector telescope, the **Extremely Large Telescope** in Chile, is due for completion in 2024. Its primary mirror will be **39.3 metres** in diameter.

Lens

Focal point

Secondary mirror

Primary mirror

Light from object

SEEING MICROBES

Light microscopes can reveal the details of tiny bacteria that are just a few **millionths** of a metre across.

SEEING ATOMS

The most powerful microscopes of all are **atomic force microscopes (AFMs)**. These do not collect light, but detect the movement of a very sharp point over an object to give a 3D impression of the object's surface. AFMs can see down to the scale of individual atoms and molecules just **trillionths** of a metre across.

HUBBLE TELESCOPE

The Hubble Space Telescope was launched in 1990. It has a mirror that is **2.4 metres** across and is designed to collect light from objects that are billions of light years away. From its place in orbit, it is high above the atmosphere and away from moving air currents that can distort images. It has taken pictures of **galaxies** that are **13.2 billion light years** away. Since light takes that amount of time to reach us on Earth, we see those galaxies as they were 13.2 billion years ago, when the Universe was only about **600 million** years old.

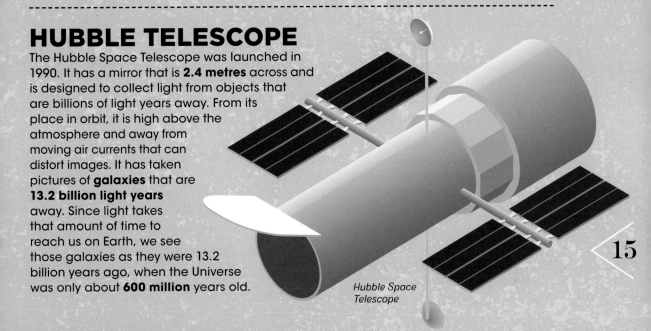

Hubble Space Telescope

15

LONG WAVES

Radio telescopes collect long radio waves from space using dishes and focus them onto a central receiver. The world's largest filled-aperture (full dish) radio telescope is the **Five Hundred Metre Aperture Spherical Telescope (FAST)** in China. Its dish is the size of 30 football pitches.

x 30 football pitches

500 m
FAST
China
(largest)

305 m
ARECIBO
Puerto Rico
(second-largest)

SHORT WAVES

Telescopes used in astronomy include X-ray and gamma ray space telescopes, which study some of the most powerful, energetic and mysterious objects in the Universe, including black holes, active galaxies and supernovae.

WHAT IS SOUND?

Sounds are caused by vibrations travelling through air or other substances. We have super-sensitive sound-detecting sensors on each side of our heads that can convert these vibrations into the noises we hear – our ears!

SOUND QUALITY

Volume is how loud or quiet the sound is.

Pitch is how low or high the sound is.

Timbre is the quality of the sound and tells us what the sound is, whether it's the crash of thunder or the squeak of a mouse.

WAVES THROUGH THE AIR

Sounds travel as waves. How quickly these waves vibrate is called the frequency and this determines the pitch of the sound. Frequency is measured using units called **hertz** (Hz). **1 kilohertz** (kHz) is 1,000 Hz, while **1 megahertz** (MHz) is a million hertz.

Amplitude
This is the height of the sound wave. Loud sounds have a large amplitude with tall peaks, while quiet sounds have a small amplitude and short peaks.

Wavelength
This is the distance between two peaks in the waves.

Frequency
This is the number of times the sound waves vibrate each second and it determines the pitch. High-pitched sounds vibrate many times per second and a have a high frequency. The opposite is true for low-pitched sounds.

DIFFERENT SHAPES

The shape of a sound wave determines its timbre. The purer the sound, the fewer lumps and bumps the wave will have.

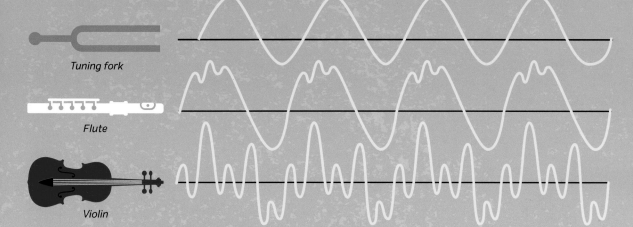

Tuning fork

Flute

Violin

INTO THE EAR

Your ear is an amazingly complicated organ. Sound waves undergo a series of transformations as they pass through the ear. Finally, the ear sends a signal to the brain to tell it what it is hearing.

Outer ear

1. *The outer ear collects sound waves and channels them through the ear canal.*

7. *The nerve signals travel along the auditory nerve to the brain, which interprets the sound.*

Ossicles

Ear canal

Auditory nerves

Eardrum

Oval window

Cochlea

6. *As the waves travel through the cochlea, they cause tiny hairs to move back and forth, which triggers nerve signals.*

2. *At the end of the ear canal, the eardrum vibrates as the sound waves hit it.*

3. *The eardrum is attached to three tiny bones, the ossicles, which transmit and magnify the vibrations.*

4. *The ossicles vibrate against a small oval window.*

5. *When the oval window vibrates, it sends waves through fluid inside the spiral-shaped cochlea.*

Sound wave

OSSICLES

The three ossicles in the ear are the smallest bones in the body, just a few millimetres across.

This coin has a diameter of 26.5 mm

Ossicles

LOUDEST

Cover your ears as these are some of the loudest sounds ever made! And while some machines and vehicles can produce really loud noises, the natural world can make the loudest sounds of all.

DECIBELS

The loudness of sounds is measured using the **decibel scale**. The quietest sound humans can hear is at 0 decibels (dB), but there are sounds even quieter than that with a negative decibel value. Sounds become quieter the farther away you are from the source of the sound.

0 dB	10 dB	20 dB	30 dB	40 dB	50 dB	60 dB	70 dB	80 dB	90 dB	100 dB	110 dB	120 dB	130 dB	140+ dB
		VERY FAINT		FAINT		MODERATE TO QUIET	LOUD		VERY LOUD			EXTREMELY LOUD		THRESHOLD OF PAIN

18

QUIETEST → LOUDEST

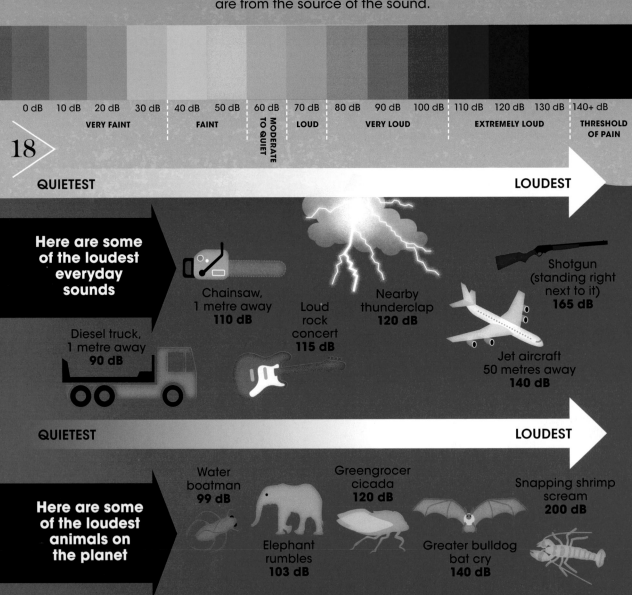

Here are some of the loudest everyday sounds

Diesel truck, 1 metre away **90 dB**

Chainsaw, 1 metre away **110 dB**

Loud rock concert **115 dB**

Nearby thunderclap **120 dB**

Shotgun (standing right next to it) **165 dB**

Jet aircraft 50 metres away **140 dB**

QUIETEST → LOUDEST

Here are some of the loudest animals on the planet

Water boatman **99 dB**

Elephant rumbles **103 dB**

Greengrocer cicada **120 dB**

Greater bulldog bat cry **140 dB**

Snapping shrimp scream **200 dB**

Clouds of hot ash

SHOCK WAVES

On 27 August 1883, the volcano **Krakatoa** in Indonesia exploded with a force of **10,000 hydrogen** bombs. The explosion was heard 5,000 km away, and registered **172 decibels** up to 160 km away.

Super hot volcanic rock

Lava flow

Krakatoa was so loud, it ruptured eardrums of people **60 km** away.

NOISY OCEAN

The loudest sounds ever recorded were made through water. **Water is denser than air**, which means that it can carry bigger sound waves. The loudest animal of all is the sperm whale, whose clicks have been measured at **230 decibels**.

A sperm whale uses its huge head to create deafening clicks

SOFTEST

These sounds are at the quiet end of the decibel scale. Some of them make a whisper sound like a rock concert!

QUIET PLEASE!

How loud we hear a sound depends on both the energy contained in the sound wave and on the wave's frequency. As the frequency increases, sounds start to become more and more faint, until eventually they entirely disappear. Children can usually hear sounds of a higher frequency than adults.

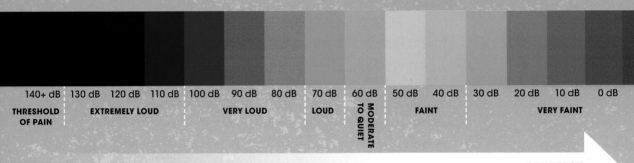

140+ dB	130 dB	120 dB	110 dB	100 dB	90 dB	80 dB	70 dB	60 dB	50 dB	40 dB	30 dB	20 dB	10 dB	0 dB
THRESHOLD OF PAIN	EXTREMELY LOUD			VERY LOUD			LOUD	MODERATE TO QUIET	FAINT		VERY FAINT			

LOUDEST → **QUIETEST**

Here are some of the quietest everyday sounds

Normal conversation
60 dB

Floor fan
50 dB

Refrigerator fan
40 dB

Pin hitting the floor **15 dB**

Whisper
30 dB

Watch ticking
20 dB

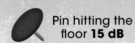

Leaves rustling
10 dB

Average threshold of human hearing
0 dB

BROWNIAN MOTION

The quietest sound possible is the sound of **Brownian motion**, which is the random movement of molecules inside a **gas** or **liquid** as they bump into one another. It is around **-24** decibels. Our ears contain liquid. If we could hear Brownian motion, our ears would deafen themselves with their own noise!

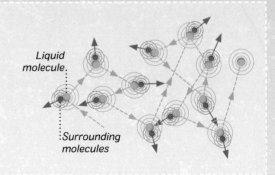

Liquid molecule

Surrounding molecules

EERIE SILENCE

Anechoic chambers are rooms that are specially designed to be extra quiet. The angles on the walls stop any sounds from echoing. These special rooms are used to carry out experiments and test audio equipment. Humans experience the chambers as total silence, and many people find this very unpleasant!

In an anechoic chamber, it is possible to detect sounds below

-0 dB

These include the sounds of a maggot wriggling, a centipede crawling or a snail munching on a leaf.

YOUNG EARS

Children generally have more sensitive ears than adults and young children can hear sounds as quiet as **-10 decibels**.

A cat's super-sensitive ears can hear sounds as quiet as **-20 dB**.

HIGH PITCH

While many animals use sounds that are too high-pitched for us to hear in order to find food (or avoid being eaten!), humans have been able to employ these unhearable sounds to help with medicine and treating people.

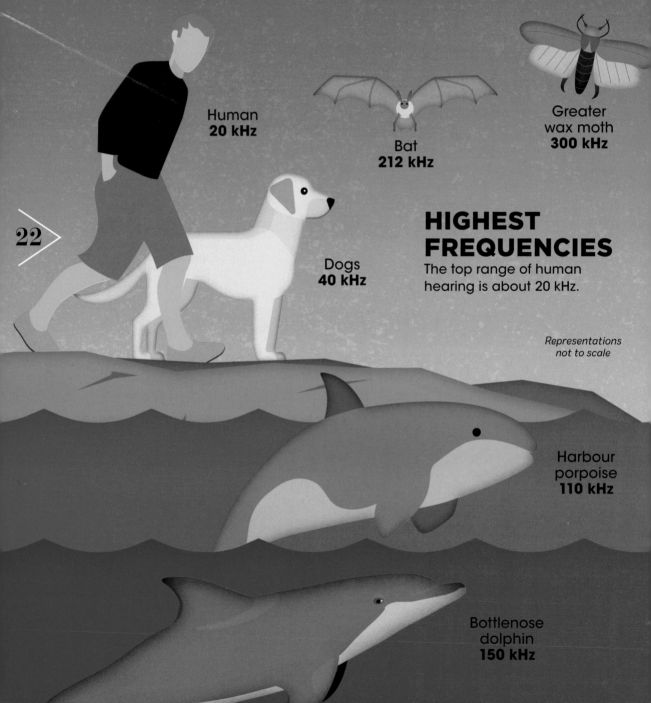

Human
20 kHz

Bat
212 kHz

Greater wax moth
300 kHz

Dogs
40 kHz

HIGHEST FREQUENCIES
The top range of human hearing is about 20 kHz.

Representations not to scale

Harbour porpoise
110 kHz

Bottlenose dolphin
150 kHz

HIGH-PITCHED HUNTING

Bats and dolphins produce and hear high-pitched sounds in order to pinpoint their prey while hunting. This is known as echolocation.

1. The bat produces high-pitched sounds.

Moth

2. The sound bounces off prey as echoes.

3. The bat detects the echoes and uses them to calculate the distance to and movement of the prey.

4. Some moths are able to detect the high-pitched frequencies used by bats to avoid becoming their next meal.

SEEING INSIDE

Doctors use very high-pitched sounds to see inside our bodies. Ultrasound scanners produce sounds with frequencies usually between **1** and **30 MHz** (megahertz), which can produce an image of the inside of a person, such as a developing foetus inside a mother, without having to cut anyone open.

1. An ultrasound machine produces high-frequency sounds.

4. The probe detects reflected sound waves.

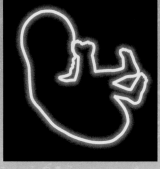

5. The machine works out the distance each echo travels and uses this to build up a picture of what's inside.

2. Sounds travel through the body.

3. Sound waves are reflected.

LOW PITCH

At the other end of the sound spectrum are noises that are too low-pitched for humans to hear – these are known as infrasound. Many animals use them to communicate with each other over huge distances and they are also produced by some of the most violent events on the planet.

LOWEST FREQUENCIES

The lowest range of human hearing is about 20 Hz.

Giraffe
11 Hz

Elephant
17 Hz

Human
20 Hz

Sumatran rhinoceros
3 Hz

Representations not to scale

Humpback whale
20-24 Hz

RUMBLE IN THE JUNGLE

Elephants make low-pitched rumbling sounds that can travel for more than **10 km**. Other elephants can detect these **vibrations** through their feet.

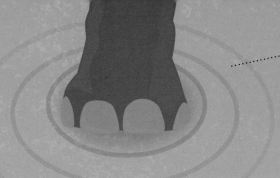

Elephants detect vibrations in the ground with sensory cells in their feet.

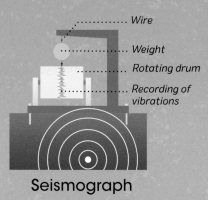

Wire

Weight

Rotating drum

Recording of vibrations

Seismograph

Pacific Ocean

Chile

DESTRUCTIVE VIBRATIONS

A **seismograph** records the low-pitched sounds made by earthquakes. The more violent the earthquake is, the greater the amplitude of the waves on the seismograph. The most violent earthquake ever recorded took place in Chile in 1960. The vibrations caused a huge wave, called a tsunami, to race across the Pacific Ocean, devastating islands thousands of kilometres from the centre of the earthquake.

Thunder produces low pitched rumbles, usually between

20–120 Hz.

But sometimes it produces infrasound frequencies we can't hear.

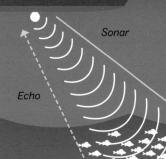

Sonar

Echo

Fishermen use **sonar** to locate shoals of fish. Sonar equipment makes sound waves that travel though water and bounce off objects. Sonar can use both high- and low-pitched sounds.

NOISY OCEAN

The songs made by humpback whales can, in theory, travel more than **2,500 km** through the water. However, the **interference** caused by the sounds of ships has limited the range of these calls. The oceans are noisy places!

SPEED OF
SOUND

Sound travels by passing vibrations from one molecule to the next. How quickly sound travels (the 'speed of sound') depends on the state of the substances it is moving through. Sounds travel much more quickly through some substances than others.

SPEED OF SOUND

Substances that are liquid or solid have more densely packed molecules than those in air. This allows the transfer of sound vibrations to take place at a greater speed. Hotter substances have more rapidly moving molecules, which also speeds up sounds.

At 20 °C, the **speed of sound through air** is 343 metres per second (m/s) (1 km in 2.91 seconds).

The **speed of sound through water** is 1,484 m/s (4.3 times faster than through air).

The **speed of sound through iron** is 5,120 m/s (15 times faster than through air).

The **speed of sound through diamond** is 12,000 m/s (35 times faster than through air).

X-43A (world's fastest aircraft)

ABOVE THE CLOUDS

As you move through the atmosphere, the speed of sound changes as the air pressure and temperature varies. The colder the air, the slower the sound.

Commercial airliner

Altitude	Temperature	Speed of sound
29,000 metres (X-43A)	-48°C	301 m/s
11,000–20,000 metres (airliner)	-57°C	295 m/s

DOPPLER EFFECT

As an object moves, it produces a sound effect called the Doppler effect, where the frequency of sound waves in front of the object are higher than those behind it. This is why the siren of a fire engine changes pitch as it passes by.

Sound waves bunch together

If an object is moving away from you, sound waves are stretched out, making the pitch lower.

If an object is moving towards you, sound waves are compressed, pushing the pitch up.

SONIC BOOM

At the speed of sound, the object catches up with the sound waves and they bunch up in front of it, forming a shockwave. When the object goes **supersonic** (faster than the speed of sound), it leaves sound waves behind it, causing them to fan out in a cone shape, and produces a sonic boom. From the ground, the sonic boom sounds like a loud crack of thunder.

Sounds cannot travel through space, because there are no

MOLECULES

(air or otherwise) to transfer the wave.

Pressure waves of air flowing off an aeroplane

Sound waves fan out in a cone.

Subsonic

Speed of sound

Supersonic

MUSICAL EXTREMES

Whether they're high- or low-pitched, loud or quiet, different notes are combined together to produce the wide range of music that has been written and performed over thousands of years.

LOW NOTES

These instruments play notes so low that we can only just hear them.

The lowest note on a **double bass** has a frequency of **34 Hz**.

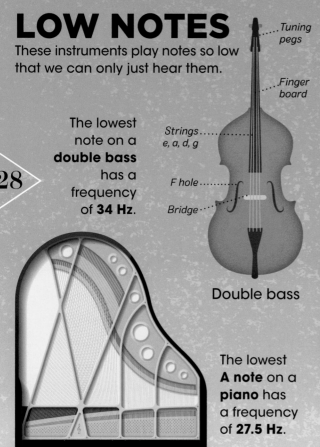

Tuning pegs

Finger board

Strings
e, a, d, g

F hole

Bridge

Double bass

Some **pipe organs** can play notes at a frequency of just **8 Hz**. The lowest notes that humans can actually hear is **20 Hz**, so we can only 'hear' these notes because they cause other notes to vibrate; an effect called **harmonics**.

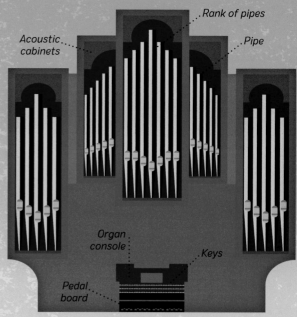

Rank of pipes

Pipe

Acoustic cabinets

Organ console

Keys

Pedal board

Pipe organ

The lowest **A note** on a **piano** has a frequency of **27.5 Hz**.

A note

HIGH NOTES

The top **pitch** of a **human's** voice is about 2,000 Hz (2 kHz). A **piccolo** can play the highest frequency notes out of all woodwind instruments, reaching up to 5.2 kHz.

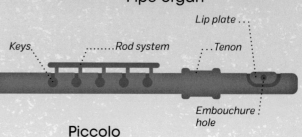

Keys

Rod system

Tenon

Lip plate

Embouchure hole

Piccolo

SHATTERING GLASS

In 2015, rock singer Jamie Vendera broke a **wine glass** with his voice. He sustained a single note at 105 decibels, and the power of the **vibrations** shattered the glass.

Shards of glass

LOUDEST INSTRUMENT

The loudest musical instrument ever built is the **Boardwalk Hall Auditorium Organ** in Atlantic City, New Jersey, USA. This huge organ has more than **33,000 pipes**, although the exact number is unknown.

Sound waves vibrate glass, making it shatter.

SINGING SAW

A singing saw is a musical instrument consisting of a **hand saw** played with a **bow**. It produces an eerie high-pitched sound. The player changes the pitch by bending the saw. Various musicians have included a singing saw in their works, including classical composer Dmitri Shostakovich (1906–75) and rock singer Tom Waits (1949–).

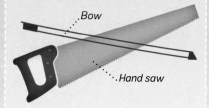

Bow

Hand saw

DEAFENING BAND

The loudest rock band ever recorded is **Manowar**, who perform at volumes up to **139 decibels**. That's as loud as a jet aircraft taking off.

GLOSSARY

ABSOLUTE MAGNITUDE
A measure of how bright an astronomical object actually is.

AMPLITUDE
How strong a wave is. In relation to sound, it describes how loud the sound is.

APPARENT MAGNITUDE
A measure of how bright an astronomical object appears in the night sky.

BLACK HOLE
A region of space where the force of gravity is so high that nothing can escape its pull, not even light.

COCHLEA
The spiral-shaped organ deep inside the ear that contains the sensors that convert sound waves into nerve signals to send to the brain.

DECIBELS
The unit that is used to measure how loud a sound is.

DOPPLER EFFECT
When the movement of an object affects the frequency of sound waves or electromagnetic radiation. For example, a police siren will appear to drop in pitch as it moves away.

ECHOLOCATION
A system used by some animals, such as bats and dolphins, to detect their surroundings as well as any potential prey. They send out high-frequency sound waves and then listen for the echoes bouncing of an object to work out where it is and where it might be moving to.

ECLIPSE
When an astronomical object, such as a planet or a moon, passes in front of a star, blocking its light.

ELECTROMAGNETIC SPECTRUM
The complete range of electromagnetic radiation, it includes invisible radio waves and microwaves as well as all the colours of visible light.

FREQUENCY
How quickly a radio wave or a sound wave vibrates.

GAMMA RAYS
A high-energy part of the electromagnetic spectrum with a very short wavelength.

INFRARED
Part of the electromagnetic spectrum that has a slightly longer wavelength than visible light, so it is invisible to humans.

INFRASOUND
Used to describe sounds whose frequencies are so low that humans cannot hear them.

LIGHT YEAR
A unit of distance. A light year is how far light travels in a year and is used to measure distances across space.

MICROWAVES
An invisible part of the electromagnetic spectrum, they are used to cook food.

OSSICLES
The name given to the smallest bones in the body. They are found deep inside the ears and they transmit sound vibrations from the eardrum and into the cochlea.

OZONE
A form of oxygen, this is a colourless gas that is found high in the atmosphere where it absorbs much of the ultraviolet radiation coming from the Sun.

PENUMBRA
An area of half-shadow that is usually found around the full shadow, or umbra.

PHOTORECEPTORS
The name given to light-sensitive cells that are found lining the back of the eye.

PITCH
The word used to describe how high or low a sound is.

PRISM
A specially shaped piece of glass or plastic that separates light into a colourful spectrum as it passes through.

RADIATION
A form of energy that is given off by an object.

RADIO WAVES
An invisible part of the electromagnetic spectrum, they are used to send signals and detect objects.

REFLECTED
When something, such as a ray of light or a sound wave, bounces off an object rather than passing through it.

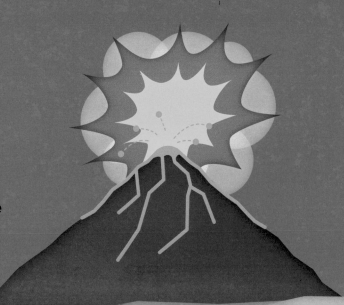

INDEX